Contents

Cello Suite No. 1
in G Major, BWV 1007

Johann Sebastian Bach
(1685–1750)

Prelude

6

Allemande

Courante

8

Sarabande

Menuet I

Menuet II

Gigue

Sonata in A Major

Edited by Janos Starker

Luigi Boccherini
(1743–1805)

Sonata in D minor

Edited by Janos Starker

Arcangelo Corelli
(1653–1713)

PRELUDIO

18

ALLEMANDA

SARABANDA

Largo

GIGA

Allegro

Sonata in D Major

Edited by Janos Starker

Pietro Locatelli
(1695–1764)

MINUETTO

animato

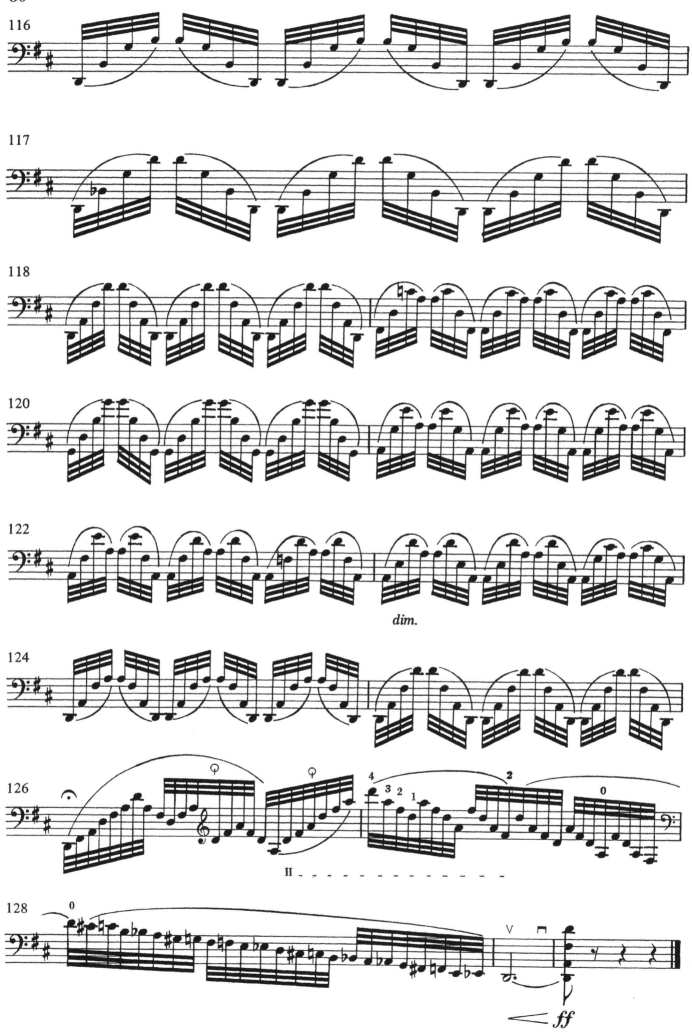

Sonata in G minor
BWV 1029

Johann Sebastian Bach
(1685–1750)

36

(cantabile)

Sonata in G Major

Edited by Janos Starker

Giovanni Battista Sammartini
(c.1700–1775)

Sonata in D minor

Realization by Analee Bacon

Alessandro Scarlatti
(1660–1725)

Largo

A tempo giusto

Fine

Sonata in E minor

Benedetto Marcello
(1686–1739)

Fine

Sonata in A minor

Antonio Vivaldi
(1678–1741)

Sonata in E Major

Edited by Janos Starker

Giuseppe Valentini
(1681–1753)